The Stuar

STATUS AND LEGACY

Edward Chaney and Godfrey Worsdale

SOUTHAMPTON CITY ART GALLERY

2001

Foreword

GODFREY WORSDALE

Some time ago I approached Professor Edward Chaney with a view to collaborating on an exhibition that would chart the rise of British painting during the eighteenth century, the general idea being to consider the contributions of the great painters who established a genuinely British school of artists that has since received international recognition of the highest order. The opportunity to bring the likes of Gainsborough, Richardson and Hogarth to Southampton City Art Gallery was of course an attractive one. As our conversations developed, however, it became increasingly apparent that the great painters of the Hanoverian period were inextricably linked to their (often immigrant) Stuart predecessors and it was within that lineage that the more intriguing enterprise was to be found. Conscious of the courtly status of Rubens and Van Dyck, indigenous artists were to develop a new sense of prowess in their own, as well as others' eyes. Further to this, the stylistic legacies that were established by those artists who served the Caroline court continued to form and inform artistic attitudes over the next century and beyond.

The history that the exhibition has eventually come to mediate is one that is informed not only by the artists involved but also by the influential patrons, connoisseurs, performers, writers and thinkers of the time. To define their centrality we quickly recognised the portrait genre as the medium in which this exhibition could most effectively clarify its purpose. It is also to this end that the self-portrait is so strongly emphasised within the selection of works.

This exhibition has come about as the result of assiduous efforts on the part of a great number of individuals and organizations, not least Southampton Institute, who have generously funded this publication. Most importantly, however, the project has been realised because of the tremendous generosity and enthusiasm of those who have lent works and contributed expertise. Above all, Professor Chaney's infectious passion for the cultural developments of those times has delivered an exhibition of unique character and remarkable insight. He and I would particularly like to thank Honor Beddard, Hugh Belsey, Lord Dacre of Glanton, Karen Hearn and James Mulraine for their catalogue entries, and John Peacock for his, as well as his insightful essay on Van Dyck in England. Thanks are also due to Paul Holberton for seeing this catalogue through the press, as well as to Ann Barnes, Ann Bukantis, Lottie Bailey, Hélène de la Rue, Roy Fox Photography, Dr Stephen Lloyd, Catharine MacLeod, Sir Oliver Millar, Dr Tim Moreton, Philip Mould, Richard Ollard, Toby Watley and Jeremy Wood.

The Stuart Portrait: *Status and Legacy*

EDWARD CHANEY

This catalogue and the exhibition for which it has been produced seek to reflect upon the character, variety and subsequent influence of Stuart portraiture. The English only began to appreciate what we now call Renaissance art when Italy and its classicizing visual culture were about to become less accessible as a consequence of the Reformation.[1] In the second half of the sixteenth century (apart from the brief respite under Mary), increasing restrictions on travel to Italy compounded the disastrous effects of iconoclasm; the excommunication of Queen Elizabeth in 1570 and the subsequent war with Spain, which then dominated most of Italy, further exacerbated an infertile artistic climate. By 1581 the Dutch artist Cornelis Ketel found the lack of patronage for anything but portrait painting so frustrating that he returned home. His biographer Van Mander wrote that, during the 1570s in England, 'he obtained many portrait commissions but none for histories, towards which his spirit was ever inclined'.[2] By the beginning of the seventeenth century, when James Stuart united a nominally Protestant Scotland and England and re-established peace with Spain, painting had become more or less synonymous with portraiture, and even this was frowned upon by the more puritanical interpreters of the Second Commandment.

Even before the Reformation, England had had to import foreigners such as Torrigiano and Benedetto da Rovezzano to create royal tombs, while Holbein set the highest standard for painted portraiture. Lucas Hornebolte's and Holbein's miniatures, with their flattened blue or decorative backgrounds, were succeeded by those of Lavina Teerlinc. Their combined legacy encouraged Nicholas Hilliard to develop this refined and essentially private art form, which was continued into the Stuart period by the French-born Isaac Oliver and his son Peter, and by John Hoskins and his son, also John, and nephew, Samuel Cooper, who restored to the genre the quality of Holbein's exquisitely heightened realism, enhanced by an almost Romantic empathy.

With John Hoskins (limner to Charles I) and Cooper (who became limner to Charles II) we arrive at the age of Van Dyck, who swept away the last vestiges of the Jacobethan 'costume piece' with that magnificent yet individualized flourish which no other artist has ever quite equalled [fig. 1]. Both Hoskins and Cooper miniaturized his work, the latter's earliest signed picture being a portrait 'in little' of Van Dyck's 'dangerous' mistress, Margaret Lemon [fig. 2]. Under James I, albeit largely thanks to his crypto-Catholic consort, Anne of Denmark, and their sons, Prince Henry and Charles, the visual arts began to prosper as never before. Between the premature death of Prince Henry in 1612 and the emergence of Charles in the 1620s as the greatest ever royal patron and connoisseur, the collector Earl of Arundel pioneered the art-focussed Grand Tour, choosing as his *cicerone* Inigo Jones [no. 23], who designed the first great neo-classical buildings in England and

1. See Sir Henry Wotton, *A Panegerik of King Charles* (London, 1644), pp. 103-4: 'Italy (the great mother of elegant arts) or at least (after the Grecians) the principal nurse, may seem by your magnificence to be translated into England'; cf. E. Chaney, *The Evolution of the Grand Tour*, 2nd edn (London, 2000), passim.

2. Karen Hearn ed., *Dynasties: Painting in Tudor and Jacobean England 1530-1630* (Tate Gallery, London, 1995), p. 112.

Fig. 1
Sir Anthony van Dyck
Lord John Stuart and his Brother Lord Bernard Stuart, c.1638
Oil on canvas, 242.5 × 148.5 cm
National Gallery, London

advised his patrons on their picture collections.

Arundel made contact with Rubens as early as 1612 and began importing both art and artists at around the same time. Soon after their return from Italy, Arundel invited the Delft-based Daniel Mijtens to come to England and portray him and his formidable wife against backdrops of sculpture and portraits respectively. It was probably the Arundels, rather than Lord Purbeck,[3] who invited Van Dyck to England in the autumn of 1620, the Countess having met him in July when she was painted by Rubens in Antwerp. Within weeks of his arrival, the twenty-one-year-old Van Dyck had demonstrated his superiority to Mijtens with the portrait of Arundel that is now in the J. Paul Getty Museum. In the following year Arundel sent Van Dyck to Italy, where he joined the Countess's entourage.

3. D. Howarth, 'The Arrival of Van Dyck in England', *Burlington Magazine*, CXXXII (1990), pp. 70-9. If Purbeck (the Marquess of Buckingham's brother) was indeed responsible for the invitation, Van Dyck's *Continence of Scipio* could equally well refer to Purbeck's marriage to the daughter of Sir Edward Coke, which was at least as controversial as that between Buckingham and the Earl of Rutland's Catholic daughter.

Charles and Buckingham followed Arundel's example, all three collecting and having themselves portrayed by Rubens and Van Dyck (both of whom were knighted), as well as by Dutch artists such as Mijtens, Cornelius Johnson and Honthorst. Even the superior genre of history painting (secular subjects replacing religious ones) made some progress under Charles I, though Honthorst's masque-like *Apollo and Diana* (Hampton Court) featured portraits of Charles, Henrietta Maria, Buckingham and his wife, the two latter conceivably echoing an earlier appearance in Van Dyck's *Continence of Scipio* (Christ Church, Oxford) and more certainly in his extraordinary *Venus and Adonis* (private collection). Van Dyck raised the conventionally low status of portraiture not merely in conversation pieces but even in his single portraits, treating them as allegories accompanied by subsidiary figures or as symbols, as in the magnificent *Venetia Digby as Prudence* (National Portrait Gallery) or less complicatedly in *Lady Mary Villiers and Lord Arran* (North Carolina Museum of Art).

Fig. 2
Samuel Cooper
*Margaret Lemon, c.*1635
Watercolour on vellum,
oval, 10.1 × 7.6 cm
Fondation Custodia (collection F. Lugt), Institut néerlandais, Paris

Like the Reformation, the Long Parliament and consequent Great Rebellion represented another major setback for the visual arts. The disgruntled Orazio Gentileschi had already died, buried under the high altar of Somerset House chapel, while his daughter Artemisia and assorted Dutch rivals returned to their respective homes. Van Dyck died in 1641, whilst arranging to move to Paris, and was buried in St Paul's Cathedral. In 1642 Charles and his Catholic consort retreated to Oxford, where Van Dyck's greatest English successor, William Dobson, portrayed the increasingly beleaguered Royalists with more realism than had his master [no. 10]. After Dobson's death towards the end of the Civil Wars, artistic uncertainty reflected the political chaos, but settled somewhat under the relatively tolerant (post-Parliamentary) personal rule of Oliver Cromwell. At the popular end of the market was the engraving of the martyred Charles I in William Marshall's frontispiece to the *Eikon Basilike*, Milton's 'image for the doting rabble'. This went through 35 editions in its first year of publication, providing the foundation for a nostalgia that haunts members of the Royal Stuart Society even today. In Scotland in 1651, Charles II distributed thirteen miniatures of himself to persuade prominent supporters to fight for the reinstatement of his father's throne.

Like the medallists Thomas and Abraham Simon, however, Peter Lely (who painted the latter), Robert Walker and the Roman Catholic John Michael Wright worked for whichever establishment prevailed during and after the Interregnum. In the 1640s Lely befriended the Cavalier poet Richard Lovelace, who eulogized the 'clouded majesty' expressed in his portrait of Charles I in captivity at Hampton Court greeting the Duke of York (Northumberland Collection), whilst deploring the 'un-understanding' and 'transalpine barbarous neglect' accorded Lely's pastorals in the style of Polenburch. But it was Lovelace who became a true victim of neglect, dying after two periods in prison in 1658, whilst Lely prospered by concentrating on portraiture, producing virile images of Cromwell (though probably derived from Cooper's more precise miniature), as well as portraying Parliamentarians such as Sir Edward Massey or the regicidal Sir Henry Vane. Meanwhile he took advantage of the sales of the late King's goods, acquiring a Veronese (which he sold on to the King of Spain), a Tintoretto, a Breenburch and (via Robert Houghton) Van Dyck's *Cupid and Psyche*, which he was obliged to return at the Restoration. The meritocratic Charles II nevertheless employed Lely as Van Dyck's successor in the role of Principal Painter, to portray himself, his family, courtiers and mistresses, both clothed and naked, occasionally featuring their illegitimate offspring as cupids.[4]

Robert Walker [no. 11] had painted the nominally Royalist (but far from Cavalier) John Evelyn, but also depicted Cromwell, his son-in-law Ireton, the Parliamentary naval commander Richard Deane, John Hampden, Sir Arthur Haselrig and the Round-headed Hutchinsons, almost all in poses cribbed from Van Dyck. Wright, who had lived and worked in Italy and the Spanish Netherlands, returned home in 1656, where he soon became 'greate with Catholique and heretique [ie Protestant] ladyes, who hath power at that court'.[5] The 'court' was that of the Cromwells, Oliver and Richard, and Wright indeed painted Oliver's favourite daughter, Elizabeth Claypole, as well as the gentleman architect Sir William Bruce, who played a significant role in the Restoration [no. 14]. Charles II commissioned Bruce to rebuild Holyrood House just as he asked Lely's friend Hugh May to modernize Windsor Castle. In Bruce's case the commission came via his friend Lord Lauderdale, whose wife, Elizabeth Dysart, was Bruce's cousin, and who were both painted by Lely. Lely also painted a portrait of himself and May with a view of Windsor Castle in the background.[6]

Though he had begun by imitating Polenburch, Lely's emulation of Van Dyck, whose pictures he continued to collect, climaxed a year before he died, when he, too, was knighted. His 'stately' self-portrait had been acquired by Charles II, just as self-portraits not only by gentlemen such as Van Dyck [no. 17] and Rubens but also by Artemisia Gentileschi and Mijtens had been acquired by Charles I, who, like Arundel, excepted artists from his otherwise hierarchical inclinations. It was not just in Holland, where Rembrandt painted at least one self-portrait a year, and not merely for his own gratification, that there was an expanding market for this genre. The young artist might embark on a portrait of himself as his most convenient (and cheapest) model, but the act of self-portraiture encourages a spirit of introspection or psychological enquiry. Dobson and Isaac Fuller produced at least three each, with clients as well as posterity in mind. The steady rise in the status of the artist is epitomized in the formation, by the Florentine Grand Duke's brother, Leopoldo de' Medici, of the largest collection of self-portraits in the world. Indicative of the superior status of art in Florence on the eve of the Stuart period was the 1602 decree which proscribed the export of the works of eighteen named painters,

4. Both mistresses and offspring were given Duchies. When Lely died there were no less than twelve portraits of the Duchess of Cleveland (Lady Castlemaine) in his studio; see David Piper, *The English Face*, ed. Malcolm Rogers (London, 1992), p. 117, and *Painted Ladies: Women at the Court of Charles* II (NPG, London, 2000). At the popular end of the market, engravings of Lady Castlemaine were the pin-ups of the day. Meanwhile, Charles II owned a Lely nude, probably of Nell Gwyn, that he kept behind a sliding panel, painted with a landscape by Dankerts.

5. M.V. Hay, *The Blairs Papers (1603–1660)* (London, 1929), p. 199.

6. Oliver Millar, *Sir Peter Lely 1618–1680* (NPG, London, 1978), p. 67.

starting with Michelangelo. Indicative of the consensus which categorized portraits as an inferior genre is that they, together with landscapes and small devotional works 'to place above the bed', were exempted from the decree.[7] Symbolic of England's 'catching up' with the Medici, however, is that Leopoldo's nephew, the future Grand Duke Cosimo III, sat to Samuel Cooper and commissioned portraits by Lely during and after his 1669 visit to this country.[8]

From the time of the Restoration the demand for portraits multiplied, even if their quality cannot be said to have improved proportionately. The popular treatise *Polygraphice*, first published in 1675, advised on the 'correct' disposition of portraits of royalty, aristocrats, wives, special friends and famous artists, in the various rooms of what could be a middle-class house. The diarists (prose self-portraitists?) Samuel Pepys and John Evelyn [no. 8] were typical in commissioning and hanging portraits of themselves and of family and friends in dining rooms, parlours and bedrooms. Lord Clarendon furnished his Piccadilly mansion with a huge collection of portraits, including many of the 'characters' he portrayed in his historical writings.[9] In around 1680, the year of Lely's death, John Riley painted an older and even uglier Lord Lauderdale (Northumberland Collection), but he also painted James II's ninety-five-year-old housemaid and an Oxford scullion, implicitly displaying a degree of defiance in the face of the theorists' condescension towards portraiture. Riley's pupils included Jonathan Richardson, who, with his son, practised and wrote on the virtues of portraiture, even while the influential Lord Shaftesbury disparaged 'face-painting ... as requiring no liberal knowledge, genius, education, converse, manners, moral-science, mathematics, optics, but merely practical and vulgar. Therefore not deserving honour, gentility, knighthood conferred (Glance at Sir Kneller).'[10]

Arriving in England four years before the death of Lely, having trained in Amsterdam and Italy, Godfrey Kneller was successful even beyond Rubens, Van Dyck and Lely in not merely being knighted (in 1692) but in becoming the first painter to receive a baronetcy, one of the first acts of George I in May 1715. Kneller's attempt to rival Lely's so-called Windsor Beauties with his oval-headed Hampton Court equivalent, however, could be said to have failed in proportion to the extent he had moved further from Van Dyck's combination of elegance and individualized realism. There is somewhat greater psychological depth, as well as 'polish' and 'politeness', in his forty-two portraits of almost identically bewigged fellow Whigs for the Kit-Cat Club.[11] It was Kneller who presided over the first English Academy for artists, the start of a trend which, as a substitute for the master-pupil relationship, would prove a mixed blessing during the next three centuries.

If a consequence of the so-called Glorious Revolution was a period in the wilderness for an Italian Catholic painter such as Verrio, the advent of Anglo-Dutch rule in 1688 had less serious consequences than the previous Protestant revolutions. Although one of Kneller's army of assistants, Henry Peart, had specialized in copying Van Dycks and Lelys, and Kneller's only distinguished pupil, Charles Jervas, did

7. Francis Haskell, *The Ephemeral Museum* (New Haven and London, 2000), pp. 4 and 164, note 4.

8. A.M. Crinò and O. Millar, 'Sir Peter Lely and the Grand Duke of Tuscany', *Burlington Magazine*, C (1958), pp. 124–30, and A.M. Crinò, *Un Principe di Toscana in Inghilterra e in Irlanda nel 1669* (Rome, 1968).

9. See Richard Ollard, 'Clarendon and the Art of Prose Portraiture in the Age of Charles II', *Art and Patronage in the Caroline Courts*, ed. D. Howarth (Cambridge, 1993), pp. 189–201.

10. *Second Characters*, ed. B. Rand (London, 1914), p. 134–5.

11. Now in the National Portrait Gallery. See David Solkin, *Painting for Money* (New Haven and London, 1993), passim.

likewise (cf. no. 17), it was not until the Hanoverians were fully established that nostalgia for the Stuart style returned, artistic Jacobitism becoming difficult to distinguish from the real thing.[12]

Although Hogarth was born in the seventeenth century, he is usually associated with a new, more demotic 'English style', one which affected to scorn Italianate art and instead depict crowded scenes illustrating contemporary mores or condemned criminals, which were then reproduced and sold as prints. Even Hogarth, however, felt sufficiently part of the tradition established by Van Dyck, a full century after his death, to make a gilded cork model of the master's head as his shop sign.[13] His copy of Van Dyck's portrait of Inigo Jones [no. 23] is a tribute to both Stuart masters and consistent with the admiration bestowed on each by his Chiswick neighbour – and butt of his satire – Lord Burlington.

Just as Hogarth married Sir James Thornhill's daughter, Thomas Hudson married the daughter of his master, Richardson. Hudson's most accomplished pupil was Joshua Reynolds, but Reynolds himself preferred the work of Hudson's only serious rival in the 1740s, the Italianate Scotsman Alan Ramsay. Unlike Hudson, who effectively retired by the end of the 1750s, Ramsay continued to work until the end of the following decade, perhaps prompted to return to Italy in 1754 for the second of his four Grand Tours by Reynolds's triumphant return home armed with prints, drawings and an Italian assistant, Giuseppe Marchi. Reynolds studied the seventeenth-century Northern masters Rubens, Van Dyck and Lely, however, as assiduously as he did the sixteenth-century Italians, both he and the contemporary who succeeded Ramsay as his most accomplished rival, Thomas Gainsborough, posing their sitters as classical sculptures dressed in early Stuart costume. As well as owning Van Dyck's *George Gage* [no. 4], which influenced his depiction of *Garrick between Tragedy and Comedy*,[14] we know that Reynolds collected engravings after Van Dyck (the so-called *Iconography*), from which he derived many of his poses.[15] Gainsborough, who was unusual in never undertaking a Grand Tour, was both more overt in his borrowings [no. 24] and more subtle in his adaptation of Van Dyck's Titianesque *colore* to his own purposes, producing refined but far from exclusively aristocratic portraits for a more overtly English clientele in an often rural setting. Gainsborough was less concerned than Reynolds about producing grand 'historical portraits' as a way of coping with the supposed inferiority of the genre. Where Kneller had watered down Van Dyck, and Reynolds often melodramatized him, Gainsborough alone rivalled the Flemish master in his almost impressionist rendering of light falling on refined yet credible features and rich folds of fabric and delicate lace.

Gainsborough and Reynolds (who was knighted in 1769) are thought to have painted about 2000 portraits between 1750 and 1790. In the wake of Hogarth's exaggerated emphasis on individuality, these two artists, both so heavily indebted to the great tradition of Stuart portraiture, finally consolidated a level of quality in British art that could compete with the rest of Europe .[16]

12. It is only recently – in large part owing to the researches of Jane Clark – that the ambivalent position *vis à vis* Jacobitism of major patrons – from Lord Burlington to the Duke of Marlborough – has been recognized.

13. J. Uglow, *Hogarth: A Life and a World* (London, 1997), p. 238.

14. Martin Postle,'Reynolds, Shaftesbury, Van Dyck and Dobson', *Apollo*, CXXXII (1990), pp. 306–11.

15. For the Revd James Granger and the collecting of engraved historical portraits, see Marcia Pointon, *Hanging the Head: Portraiture and Social Formation in Eighteenth-Century England* (New Haven and London, 1993).

16. With this genre finally elevated beyond the range of its theorizing critics, it was now the turn of Richard Wilson and the English watercolourists, followed by Turner and Constable (who particularly admired Gainsborough), to draw on another rich, seventeenth-century tradition and elevate landscape painting as an equivalently significant yet somehow particularly British genre. The British are given pioneering status in the magnificent exhibition recently at the Grand Palais, Paris, and now in Mantua: *Paysages d'Italie: Les Peintures du plein air (1780–1830)*.

Van Dyck in England

JOHN PEACOCK

Van Dyck is not regarded as one of the very greatest seventeenth-century painters – not the equal of Rubens, Poussin or Velázquez – but he was distinguished and extraordinarily influential. If one said perversely that the most famous of all Van Dycks was by Gainsborough, many people would recognise the reference to the so-called *Blue Boy*, because they have a notion of what 'Van Dyck' signifies: he is not only a powerful presence in the tradition of European painting but in a broader culture. Even so, notions of Van Dyck may vary from time to time, and from place to place. The recent exhibition to mark the quatercentenary of his birth began in Antwerp, then transferred to London; in each city it was articulated quite differently, and not only because the gallery spaces were dissimilar. In both venues it began with the small *Self-portrait* (Vienna), painted when he was fourteen or fifteen years old, a work of engaging brilliance. In Antwerp this was displayed on its own in an ample space hung with black drapes, the painting picked out by spotlights. In London it was merely the first item among many in one of the Royal Academy's largest rooms, quietly inaugurating an itinerary which culminated in a parade of King Charles's courtiers. The precociously dazzling son of Antwerp was seen as a very different figure from the celebrant of Stuart aristocracy. In spite of his cosmopolitan career, much of which was spent in his native Flanders or in Italy, with visits to Holland and France, England has always been very proprietorial about Van Dyck.

When he returned to London in 1632, to become Principal Painter to Charles I and Henrietta Maria, he added one more to the number of Continental artists, from Italy, France, the Netherlands and Germany, who were already in the employ of the Crown. Even so, he must have seemed like the spectacular bloom in his later *Self-Portrait* [no. 17], the sunflower which had arrived from the 'New World' in the previous century and invaded the gardens of Europe; and the picture does convey an amused sense of himself as an exotic interloper. But, though some of his fellow artists, and the London trade guild, the Painter-Stainers' Company, had reason to be jealous, he got on famously with the courtiers who became his patrons. Talent, early success and acquired wealth had enabled him to lead a life of conspicuous splendour, and to adopt the cultivated manners of the social élite whose portraits he painted. This theme runs through his earliest biography, by the Italian critic Bellori, who sums it up by saying that he lived in a style 'more like a prince than a painter (*più … da principe che da pittore*)', a defining phrase which Soprani, his next biographer, repeated.

It is fair to say that Van Dyck's lifestyle was not just self-indulgent, but also self-conscious and exemplary. Its context was the debate which had been going on since the previous century, especially in Italy, about the status of the visual arts, with the continued effort to argue that painting was not just a form of manual labour and therefore

Fig. 3
Sir Anthony van Dyck
Philip Herbert, 4th Earl of Pembroke and his family, 1633–4
Oil on canvas, 330 × 510 cm
Collection of the Earl of Pembroke, Wilton House

lacking in dignity, but a work of the intellect which entitled its practitioners to a corresponding social prestige. In all his self-portraits Van Dyck never shows himself with his palette and brushes: his hands are in repose or gesturing gracefully, to suggest that he is the equal of his sitters. When he depicts his fellow artists, especially for the series of prints known as the *Iconography*, he accords them the same degree of personal and social distinction as he would an aristocrat. So by the way he lived in London he was making a claim not only for himself but for the art of painting.

The response can be gauged from a letter written by the Earl of Newcastle, addressing him as 'Noble Sir': 'Next the blessing of your company and sweetness of conversation, the greatest blessing were to be an Argus or all over but one eye, so it or they were ever fixed upon that which we must call yours.'[1] Newcastle was a thinking man's grandee, a writer of poems and plays, who was also interested in scientific matters, including optics. Here he fantasizes about becoming the hundred-eyed Argus of classical mythology, or else being transformed into a pure eye (a conceit he repeated in a later poem), in order to intensify the experience of gazing at Van Dyck's portraits. He associates the artist's personal charm and social expertise with the visual gratification given by his work. This was the power that Van Dyck exercised over the British élite, then and thereafter: he made them associate visual with social pleasure.

He also made the pleasure of his work minister to their sense of self-importance, by endowing them with an air of 'natural' superiority. Among all the painters of early modern Europe, Van Dyck was the

1. Emil Schaeffer, *Van Dyck. Des Meisters Gemälde* (Stuttgart and Leipzig, 1909), pp. 514–5.

most successful in representing the aristocratic ideal described in the enormously influential *Book of the Courtier* (1527) by Baldassare Castiglione. The key to this was the quality of *sprezzatura*, or gracefully studied unself-consciousness: the courtier was to be as accomplished as possible in all the arts of peace and war, but had to perform these accomplishments without the slightest sense of effort or deliberation, so that they seemed innate. This programme has clear political implications: a ruling class can suggest that its ascendancy is not just one possible form of government, but part of the natural order. Castiglione had compared the perfect courtier to a painter, who with one nonchalantly felicitous brushstroke can show his mastery: a century after the book first appeared (it was continually reprinted and translated) Van Dyck's effortless display of technique fitted the comparison perfectly, and echoed the sense of spontaneous pre-eminence which he conferred on his sitters.

How far he idealized their personal appearance is difficult to say: contemporary reports are scanty and variable. His friend Sir Kenelm Digby wrote that his portraits were not flattering: 'The best faces are seldom satisfied with Van Dyck'. This is confirmed by the Countess of Sussex, whose face was not of 'the best': she complained that her cheeks were made to look fat and distended 'like one of the winds puffing – but truly I think it is like the original'. By contrast, Henrietta Maria's niece thought Van Dyck had glamourized the Queen excessively. We have to remind ourselves that notions of appearance depend on cultural contexts, such as Castiglione's widely diffused ideas about aristocratic conduct; and the 'look' that Van Dyck devised for the Stuart courtiers was more than a visual phenomenon.

Its origins may lie in his first visit to Whitehall in the winter of 1620, to work for James I. Two paintings which survive from this brief stay foreshadow the work which he produced after his return to the service of Charles I in the 1630s. For the Marquess of Buckingham he painted *The Continence of Scipio* (Christ Church, Oxford), a complex scene from the wars between Rome and Carthage; and for the Earl of Arundel a sober but finely executed half-length portrait (J. Paul Getty Museum). The *Scipio* belonged to the genre of 'history painting', as it later came to be known: contemporaries called it simply 'history' or 'story'. However, the two main figures look like portraits of Buckingham and his wife, so that King James's arriviste favourite (who not long before had been plain George Villiers) is installed in the glorious chronicle of classical history. In this way his figure resonates like that of the simply portrayed Arundel, a nobleman of genuinely ancient lineage. When Van Dyck resettled in London from 1632 he again received commissions for 'histories' (the category included religious pictures and allegories) from a few adventurous patrons; but the main demand was for portraits. His previous practice in Antwerp had depended on both genres. Now some of the untapped inventiveness appropriate to grand narrative works was channelled into portraiture.

This infusion of portraiture with implicit narrative can be seen as early as *George Gage* [no. 4], but reappears intensified in the double

Fig. 4
Cornelius Johnson
The Capel Family, c.1640
Oil on canvas, 160 × 259.1 cm
National Portrait Gallery

portraits of the Caroline period, such as *George Digby and William Russell* (Althorp). It is most evident in portraits of families. An early biographer praised these for showing 'the greatest intelligence in the placement of figures and groups, so that the composition is as harmonious and dignified as possible'.[2] This formalistic compliment glosses over the latent drama. Tolstoy remarked on the benign sameness of happy families and the oddity of unhappy ones; but we admire *War and Peace* because historical turmoil is interwoven with family strife. Van Dyck's families may be harmoniously composed in visual terms, but these patterns can rest on a matrix of subtle conflict.

The ambiguous impact of such works in England is seen in a comparison of *The Herbert Family* (now the great showpiece of the Double Cube Room at Wilton House) [fig. 3] with Cornelius Johnson's *Capel Family* [fig. 4]. Van Dyck's example probably stimulated the more modest Johnson to work on such a scale. He includes in the background Lord Capel's new formal garden at Little Hadham, using it as a visual metaphor for the grid of family relationships and the balance of nature and nurture in human upbringing. As a result, however, the image of the family comes across as overly topographical; and the appeal of the picture (which has some beautiful passages of painting) lies in its refusal to dramatize. In the Van Dyck the interaction of the figures, which contemporaries would have known how to read, is all-important. The Earl of Pembroke, Lord Chamberlain, presides, lightly holding his staff of office; beside him the Countess, who was estranged from her husband, sits absently impassive. He gestures towards his future daughter-in-law, Lady Mary Villiers, as she mounts the dais: she

2. Ed. Erik Larsen, *La Vie, les ouvrages et les élèves de Van Dyck. Manuscrit inédit des Archives du Louvre. Par un auteur anonyme* (Académie Royale de Belgique. Mémoires de la classe des Beaux-Arts. Collection in 8° – 2e Série, Tome XIV, Fascicule 2, 1975; Brussels, 1975), p. 109.

was entering the family with royal approval and an appreciably large dowry. On the right is his eldest child, Lady Anne; her husband the Earl of Carnarvon stands slightly lower, on two adjacent steps. The elegant pose has a meaning in the *drame de famille*: when she married him he was a mere baron, and the King allowed her to retain her precedence as an earl's daughter instead of sinking to that of a baroness and stepping down in the social scale to her husband's level. These are some of the major and minor themes in Van Dyck's portrayal of a powerful aristocratic family. He accentuates their power by attributing to domestic and dynastic concerns the momentousness and mystique of a 'history'.

In the individual portraits which form the bulk of his English output there is the same effort to romanticize and magnify the sitters. In the absence of others with whom to interact, they commune with themselves. Van Dyck had learnt from Venetian Renaissance painting how to endow his figures with subjectivity, with the sense of a richly self-conscious interior life. In combination with a noble deportment, opulent clothes and an impressive setting this quality becomes very potent, reinforcing the idea that the Caroline élite were 'naturally' entitled to their exalted position.

This view of Van Dyck connects him, perhaps unexpectedly, with Hogarth at the other end of our chosen period. Hogarth's treatment of personality and social relations has often been compared with the 'rise of the novel' in the eighteenth century. Insofar as the novel superseded the epic, recounting the fortunes of individuals and families instead of the vicissitudes of nations and empires, Van Dyck's grand narration of the all too human traits of his early Stuart aristocrats may have a place in the cultural process which assisted its development.

His legacy to British painting was not easy to assimilate. The one contemporary who understood Van Dyck's pictorial style was the miniaturist Samuel Cooper. His earliest signed work is a homage to the senior artist: a portrait [fig. 2] of *Margaret Lemon*, the painter's mistress, in a brilliant imitation of his style. As she is dressed in male costume, Cooper's picture wittily identifies itself as a travesty, while being carried out with a grace and intelligence worthy of the master. It was to be some time before official, large-scale portraiture managed to transform and assimilate Van Dyck's achievement. The great political crisis which extended over two decades following his death in 1641 meant that no future artist could represent a governing regime with the kind of potency that he had conferred on the Personal Rule of Charles I. Dobson's portraits of the Royalists at war have their own short-lived distinction; Lely's images of the second Caroline court show the impossibility of emulating his predecessor. In a longer perspective, eighteenth-century painters found ways of coming to terms with him. Reynolds pursued the project of introducing 'history' into portraiture, applying the lessons of Van Dyck's *Pembroke Family*, for example, to his group portrait of the Duke of Marlborough at Blenheim, but in a more programmatic fashion. Gainsborough, fascinated by Van Dyck's style, as we can see in his avid paraphrase [no. 24] of *Lord Bernard Stuart* [fig. 1], recreated it in his own remarkable version.

1

Abraham van Blijenberch (fl. 1617–22)

Ben Jonson, c.1617

Oil on canvas, 47 × 41.9 cm
National Portrait Gallery

Roy Strong, *Tudor and Jacobean Portraits in the National Portrait Gallery*, 2 vols. (London, 1969), I, pp. 183–4

Oliver Millar, *The Age of Charles I. Painting in England 1620-1649* (London, 1972), p. 20

Blijenberch is known to have been in London between 1617 and 1621. He painted a portrait of Charles, Prince of Wales, and made designs for the royal tapestry works at Mortlake. He also painted portraits of William Herbert, 3rd Earl of Pembroke, who was a patron of Ben Jonson, and Robert Kerr, 1st Earl of Ancram, a friend of John Donne, Jonson's fellow poet. This network of relationships suggests a context for the present picture in the literary culture of the Jacobean court.

Ben Jonson (1573?–1637) was a professional dramatist and poet, employed from 1605 by Queen Anne, the wife of James I, to provide the texts of the court masques in collaboration with the designer Inigo Jones [no. 23], with whom he eventually quarrelled. He became, in effect, the first poet laureate, eventually receiving a royal pension. In one of his poems he refers self-deprecatingly to 'my ... rocky face'; Blijenberch's ostensibly realistic portrait gives a less severe account of his features.

JOHN PEACOCK

2

Sir Anthony van Dyck (1599–1641)

Portrait of a Man, c.1619–20

Oil on canvas, 125 × 88.75 cm

3

Portrait of a Woman, c.1619–20

Oil on canvas, 122.5 × 87 cm

Southampton City Art Gallery

Erik Larsen, *The Paintings of Anthony van Dyck*, 2 vols. (Freren, 1988), II, p. 32

Christopher Wright, *Renaissance to Impressionism. Masterpieces from Southampton City Art Gallery* (London, 1998), p. 90

When these pictures entered the Gallery in 1953, the sitters were thought to be the merchant Van der Heyden and his wife, but there is no evidence for this identification. However, they are typical of the young Van Dyck's portraits of the Antwerp bourgeoisie, and may be compared with the full-lengths of a merchant couple now separated between the Antwerp Museum and Broadlands (see C. Brown and H. Vlieghe, *Van Dyck 1599-1641* [Antwerp and London, 1999], pp. 119–21).

Although both canvases (especially that of the man) have sustained damage through imprudent cleaning at some time before they entered the collection, these are manifestly vigorous examples of Van Dyck's early portraiture. Husband and wife are conventionally contrasted, but the artist manages this in his own individual way. The man stands with his left arm resting on a tall chair-back over which his cloak is draped: this makes for a casually graceful disposition of his hands, emphasizes his upright posture, and (through the spreading of the cloak) increases the bulk of his figure. The curtain straight behind appears to hang heavily, and helps to push him to the front of the picture space. The overall impression is of gravity and directness. By contrast, the woman sits, so that her figure bends and recedes, leaving more space for the play of the spectator's eye, which is invited by the virtuoso painting of her gold embroidered bodice. This effect of patient allowance is emphasized by the drawing aside of the curtain and the steep recession of the architectural plinth, creating a kind of optical slipstream which draws her, and the viewer, farther into the background. While at first sight the background landscape seems perfunctory, it actually repeats the foreground in visual shorthand: the sky paraphrases the curtain, and the distant blue mountain rising from the plain mimics the woman's posture, seated but erect; there is also a metaphorical mimicry of her 'level' gaze. This use of a modest landscape background to add resonance to a portrait recurs in Van Dyck's work: one may compare the much later *Abbé Scaglia with the Virgin and Child* (National Gallery); and the technique is raised to a higher pitch of eloquence in *Lady Anne Carr, Countess of Bedford* (Petworth).

JP

4

Sir Anthony van Dyck

George Gage, 1622

Oil on canvas, 115 cm × 113.5 cm
National Gallery, London

Original unpublished Papers illustrative of the Life of ... Rubens, ed. A.N. Sainsbury (London, 1859)

Mary Hervey, *The Life, Correspondence ... Thomas Howard, Earl of Arundel* (Cambridge, 1921)

John P. Feil, *Sir Tobie Matthew and his Collection of Letters* (unpublished PhD dissertation, University of Chicago, 1962)

Oliver Millar, 'Notes on Three Pictures by Van Dyck', *Burlington Magazine* (1969), pp. 414–17

Edward Chaney, *The Grand Tour and the Great Rebellion* (Geneva, 1985), pp. 263–6

Susan Barnes, 'Van Dyck and George Gage', in *Art and Patronage in the Caroline Courts*, ed. D. Howarth (Cambridge, 1993), pp. 1–11

Edward Chaney, *The Evolution of the Grand Tour*, 2nd edn (London, 2000), passim

This early work exemplifies the nature of Van Dyck's English legacy, for it belonged to and influenced Sir Joshua Reynolds, though he supposed the central sitter to be Rubens. The current identity of the sitter was first proposed in 1969 by Sir Oliver Millar, who drew attention to the similarity between the motifs on the altar-like pedestal on which the sitter is leaning and the Gage family arms, which feature a saltire and sun in splendour. The family crest is a ram's head, though this motif is in any case common on the corners of Roman altars.

Despite its status as one of Van Dyck's earliest English portraits (after that of Arundel now in the J. Paul Getty Museum), it seems odd that one of the most extraordinary facts about the sitter is never mentioned in the literature, namely that, though he became King James's official agent in Rome, Gage was not merely a Roman Catholic but was a Catholic priest and probably a Jesuit. Though it is said that Gage's first stay in Rome was in 1623, he was in fact there in 1611, when he appears in a list of Catholics in Italy sent by Viscount Cranborne to his father, and was there again in May 1614, when he was ordained by Cardinal Bellarmine during Arundel's Grand Tour with Inigo Jones. Thanks to his extensive travels and an innate artistic talent, Gage became, along with Arundel's more or less full-time art agent, William Petty, Britain's foremost connoisseur. Gage and his intimate friend Tobie Matthew, who was certainly a Jesuit, and yet was knighted by James I, played key roles in the attempt to marry the heir to the throne, Prince Charles, to the Infanta Maria of Spain. Gage was already close to Rubens in 1617 when he began negotiating Rubens's exchange of pictures for Sir Dudley Carleton's sculpture collection. By 1620 William Trumbull's secretary wrote to Carleton that Gage 'hath more authority [over Rubens] than any man I know' (Sainsbury, p. 51). Van Dyck's portrait focusses upon Gage's enhanced expertise

in sculpture (Henry Peacham praised Gage for procuring Charles I's cast of the Borghese *Gladiator*) but he may also have been instrumental in arranging Van Dyck's first visit to England in 1620. Arundel's Italian secretary Vercellini reported to his employer on Rubens's portrait of his wife in July 1620 that Van Dyck's pictures 'are hardly less esteemed than his master's' (Hervey, p. 176); Matthew then reported to Carleton on the twenty-one-year-old artist's removal to England the following November. Within a few weeks of his arrival, Arundel had Van Dyck paint his portrait, and then sponsored the artist's journey to Italy in 1621, when he joined Lady Arundel's entourage in the Veneto. In May 1621 Gage was back in Rome, where Van Dyck probably painted this picture between February and July of 1622, immediately prior to painting the portraits of Sir Robert Shirley and his wife now at Petworth (though both Gage and Van Dyck were also in Rome during the spring of 1623). The black servant adds to the narrative element in this picture just as he does in Van Dyck's *Continence of Scipio* (Christ Church, Oxford), in both instances inviting the spectator's psychological involvement in the scene. This

portrait is probably the *'ritratto de Mr. Gage'* which is recorded as belonging to Countess of Arundel (see Mary L. Cox, 'Inventory of Pictures, etc., in the Possession of Alethea, Countess of Arundel, at the Time of her Death at Amsterdam in 1654', *Burlington Magazine*, XIX (1911), p. 286.
In April 1632 Van Dyck returned to England, initially staying with Edward Norgate, the brother-in-law of Nicholas Lanier [no. 9], whose 1628 portrait was said by Peter Lely to have been the reason Charles I invited Van Dyck to settle in the country. In around 1637 Van Dyck dedicated Vorsterman's engraving of his *Lamentation* to Gage, who by now had settled down as Lady Arundel's chaplain, in memory of 'their former dealings with each other in the City [Rome]; an eternal proof of the same love'.

EDWARD CHANEY

5

Sir Peter Paul Rubens (1577–1640)

Thomas Howard, 14th Earl of Arundel, 1629

Oil on canvas, 68.6 cm × 53.3 cm
National Portrait Gallery

Mary Hervey, *The Life, Correspondence … Thomas Howard, Earl of Arundel* (Cambridge, 1921)

Frances Huemer, *Portraits*, I (*Corpus Rubenianum Ludwig Burchard*, XIX) (London, 1977), pp. 105–7, no. 4

David Howarth, *Lord Arundel and his Circle* (London and New Haven, 1985)

Arundel probably first met Rubens in 1612 in Antwerp, whence the artist had returned after several years in Italy. These two extraordinary men followed each other's careers, both characterized by competitive collecting, with great interest. On at least two occasions Rubens borrowed motifs from Arundel's ever-growing sculpture collection, while Arundel was already trying to obtain drawings from Rubens in 1617 and had his wife painted on her way to Italy, complete with dwarf, dog and Sir Dudley Carleton, in 1620. At the same time, Arundel's Italian secretary Vercellini recommended Rubens's pupil, Van Dyck, by whom Arundel had himself painted a few months later. In January 1623 Rubens dedicated Vorsterman's print after his *Battle of the Amazons* to this *'excellentissimae heroinae'*. Largely as a result of these contacts, Rubens was commissioned to paint a self-portrait for the royal collection. Between 1625 and 1628 Rubens completed a ceiling painting and an extremely expensive equestrian portrait for Arundel's great rival the Duke of Buckingham. After Buckingham's assassination, Rubens himself came to London, representing the Habsburgs in the negotiations for peace. In August 1629 Rubens wrote admiringly of Arundel's collections. Partly as a result of the assassination of Buckingham, Arundel was said to have 'grown into great grace with the King', and moved back into his lodging at Whitehall. Despite the peace negotiations, which he supported, he chose to be portrayed by Rubens in armour, gripping his Earl Marshall's baton, his helmet at his side. The finished picture, which is now in the Isabella Stewart Gardner Museum in Boston, may have been completed in Antwerp after this no less powerful study, which is one of the most distinguished pictures in National Portrait Gallery. Certainly this was Rubens's practice in the portrait of Lady Arundel and in his contemporary study of Theodore de Mayerne. Arundel's pose is indebted to Titian's now destroyed portraits of Roman Emperors, which came to the royal collection at this time from Mantua with the rest of the Gonzaga collection.

The 1975 cleaning of the Stewart Gardner portrait revealed that the head and shoulders (those parts featured in the NPG portrait) were superbly painted by Rubens himself, while the rest was probably sketched by the master and completed by another hand. The National Gallery portrait of Arundel probably dates from a

decade later. The less finished NPG picture may be 'the old Earle of Arundels head of Rubens' which John Evelyn records being bought in June 1693 for £20 in the 'great Auction of Pictures' belonging to the Jacobite exile Lord Melford by William Glanville, the son of his sister Jane, to whom he had presented his own portrait by Arundel's servant Hendrik van der Borcht more than half a century earlier [no. 8].

Arundel's secretary, Sir Edward Walker, described him as having a countenance that was 'Majestical and grave, his Visage long, his Eyes large black and piercing; he had a hooked Nose , and some Warts or Moles on his Cheeks; his Countenance was brown, his Hair thin on his Head and Beard; he was of a stately Presence and Gate, so that any Man that saw him, though in never so ordinary Habit, could not but conclude him to be a great Person ...' (*Historical Discourses* [London, 1705], p. 221). The handling of Arundel's face is somewhat smoother and thinner in the NPG portrait than in the one in Boston. The latter, however, does not feature Arundel's double wart. The wiry hair reminds one of the water-colour and pen-and-ink portrait of Arundel in the Ashmolean Museum, Oxford, which may be in Rubens's hand. EC

6

John Hoskins (c.1595–1664)
Sir Theodore de Mayerne, 1635

Oil on canvas
Lord Dacre of Glanton

Theodore de Mayerne (né Turquet), a Huguenot born in Geneva in 1573 and educated in the Universities of Heidelberg and Montpellier, was *médicin ordinaire* of Henry IV of France. After the King's assassination in 1610, he was invited to England as physician-in-chief to James I. He soon became the most famous (and most expensive) physician there. A cosmopolitan of wide interests and courtly manners, he became the King's confidential agent in diplomatic and other non-medical matters. In 1620 he bought from the Canton of Berne the barony and castle of Aubonne in the Pays de Vaud. Charles I continued his appointment at Court but was suspicious of his political activity and forbade him to travel, but Queen Henrietta Maria was devoted to him and resisted Richelieu's attempt to replace him with a medical spy of his own. On the outbreak of the Civil War Mayerne declined to follow the King to York and stayed in London, where he died, aged 82 and enormously rich, in 1655. As a physician he was a Paracelsian and a Hermetist in theory and promoted the use of chemical remedies, but in practice he was an eclectic. His most lasting achievement was in therapy – his revival and use of the regularly recorded case histories of his patients in the manner of Hippocrates.

Mayerne was an amateur of the arts and made careful records of the techniques of the painters of his time, several of whom were his patients. He encouraged Edward Norgate to write his treatise *Miniatura* and invented enamels for Jean Petitot, who painted the miniature of him at Ham House. There are several portraits of him, the most famous being by Rubens (1630). An earlier portrait, of about 1620, probably by Paul van Somer, has recently been identified and is now in the National Portrait Gallery. My portrait was evidently painted in 1635. An engraving based on it in the British Museum is inscribed 1636 and gives Mayerne's age as sixty-three, which is correct for the period 1635–6. A note among Mayerne's manuscripts records a statement about the paintings of Holbein made by Hoskins 'while he was painting Dr Mayerne, September 1635'. This seems to establish the identity of the artist. The bust of Hippocrates, resting on a book inscribed *Hermes*, declares Mayerne's ancient masters in practice and theory.

There are two versions of this portrait. The other version belongs to the Marquess of Bath and is at his home at Longleat. Lord Bath's portrait is a palimpsest, being painted over an earlier portrait of an Elizabethan lady. From this fact I deduce that my version is the original, since a portrait commissioned by the sitter would presumably be painted on a clean canvas. Lord Bath's version is first recorded in the Longleat inventory of 1706. The owner of Longleat, the first Viscount Weymouth, had by then created a new library there and had been acquiring portraits of literary and scientific men to decorate it; so probably the portrait of Mayerne was acquired for this purpose. The provenance of my portrait is unrecorded. It was offered for sale by Christie's on 5 February 1971, but not then sold, and was subsequently acquired by me in Edinburgh.

HUGH TREVOR-ROPER

7

Style of Van Dyck
Two Young Englishmen, c.1635–40

Oil on canvas, 193.7 × 126 cm
National Gallery, London

Gregory Martin, *National Gallery Catalogues. The Flemish School c.1600–c.1900* (London, 1970), pp. 63–7

Erik Larsen, *The Paintings of Anthony van Dyck*, 2 vols. (Freren, 1988), II, p. 51

The inscription *Lord Iohn and Lord Bernard Stuart./ Sons of the Duke of Lenox* is now viewed sceptically. Those two noblemen are considered to be the subjects of a double portrait by Van Dyck formerly at Broadlands and now in the National Gallery [fig. 1]. (For Gainsborough's copy of Bernard Stuart's head, see no. 24). The present picture appears to be derived from that one, and imitates its spirited compositional scheme while misunderstanding or falling short of it in certain ways. The man on the right plants one foot on a plinth which offers no surface on which he could gain a purchase; and the architecture overall is not logically articulated. The two faces gaze into vastly separated implied distances of exaggerated scope, slackening the effect of the juxtaposed figures and the contrast between them. But even if this is Van Dyck melodramatized by an imitator or disciple, it has an obvious pictorial bravura; and one can appreciate why it used to be displayed 'upstairs' in the National Gallery before being dismissed 'downstairs' to the reserve

collection. The costumes seem quasi-theatrical, and recall Van Dyck portraits of courtiers in fancy dress. The ornamented boots of the man on the left may be compared with those worn by *Lord George Stuart, Seigneur d'Aubigny* (National Portrait Gallery) or *Sir John Suckling* (New York, Frick Collection), and his carelessly draped mantle with that of *Philip, Lord Wharton* (National Gallery of Art, Washington, D.C.).

JP

8

Hendrik van der Borcht the Younger (1614–1654)

John Evelyn, 1641

Oil on canvas, 73.7 × 60.1 cm
Private collection

Francis Springell, *Connoisseur and Diplomat* (London, 1963)

Robert Harding, 'John Evelyn, Hendrik van der Borcht and Wencelaus Hollar', *Apollo*, CXLIV (1996), pp. 39–44

The famous diarist, amateur artist and writer on gardening, printing and pollution in London John Evelyn (1620–1706) became as knowledgeable as he did in large part because he spent so much of the Interregnum on an extended European tour. Shortly before leaving, on 29 June 1641, he visited London with his sister Jane. 'The day after', he writes in his diary, 'I sate to one Vanderborcht for my Picture in Oyle which I presented to her, being her request upon my resolutions to absent myselfe from the ill face of things at home ...'. Arundel had employed Van der Borcht since encountering him in Frankfurt in 1636, having already gathered up Wenceslaus Hollar in Cologne. (Arundel probably met Van der Borcht Senior in 1613 on his way to Heidelberg with the Princess Elizabeth). While Hollar was brought home to London, Arundel sent the young Van der Borcht with William Harvey to join his art agent, William Petty, in his hunt for pictures in Florence, writing of his intention to train the youth 'to take to our pictures and collection of designs at Arundel House, he being apt to love and understand matters of art ...' (Springell, p. 101). That Evelyn also describes Van der Borcht as an excellent painter, a view corroborated by others, raises a degree of doubt about the authorship of this rather wooden portrait, though it clearly depicts Evelyn. There is another version of this portrait, depicting Evelyn holding a book (as he does forty-seven years later when painted by Kneller for Pepys holding a copy of *Sylva*), that also had a family provenance (see the exhibition catalogue, published by Sotheby's in 1986, entitled *Sussex and the Grand Tour*, p. 9). The obscure drawing Evelyn holds in this portrait perhaps depicts a melancholic David with the head of Goliath, if the lance-like object held by the youth of indeterminate gender could be read as the sword with which David decapitated the Philistine. If so this version may be later than the one he presented to his sister and may refer to the post-1642 struggle against the Puritans. In late 1642, Van der Borcht travelled down to Wotton, the Evelyns' Surrey house, and sold some pictures to Evelyn and his brother. In 1644 he was with Evelyn in Paris, visiting collections on the recommendation of Arundel. He commissioned Hollar to etch a copy of Van Dyck's *Self-Portrait with a Sunflower* [cf. no. 17], which he dedicated to Evelyn as 'a great lover of the art of painting' (for Evelyn's prints see Anthony Griffiths, 'The Etchings of John Evelyn', in D. Howarth, ed., *Art and Patronage in the Caroline Courts* [Cambridge, 1993], pp. 51-67).

EC

9

Nicholas Lanier (1588–1666)

*Self-portrait holding brush and palette, c.*1644

Oil on canvas; 66 × 58.4 cm
Music Faculty, Oxford

R.L. Poole, *Catalogue of Portraits in ... Oxford*, 2 vols. (Oxford, 1912)

Michael I. Wilson, *Nicholas Lanier: Master of the King's Music* (London, 1994)

Susan E. James, 'The Model as Catalyst: Nicholas Lanier and Margaret Lemon', *Jaarboek Koninklijk Museum voor Schone Kunsten* (Antwerp, 1999), pp. 71–89

E. Chaney, *The Evolution of the Grand Tour*, 2nd edn (London, 2000)

The melancholy which characterizes many early Stuart portraits was exacerbated by the Civil Wars and is here made explicit by a skull, which, like the one on which John Evelyn rests his hand in the slightly later, 1648, portrait by Robert Walker (NPG), rests on a manuscript, almost as if devouring it. Here the manuscript features the bars of a canon, suggesting that Lanier has resorted to painting himself because his music is no longer required. The words accompanying the canon read, *Thus. Thus. at last wee must reduced/ be to naked boanes and dust*, the whole subscribed *made and paynted by Nich: Lanier*. As Master of the King's Music Lanier remained a firm Royalist throughout the Interregnum and was thus in besieged Oxford in the 1640s, when he would have painted this and presented it to the University. He may indeed have been a

Roman Catholic, appearing as he does on a list of indicted recusants in Chiswick drawn up soon after the calling of Parliament in 1640. Lanier was also a pioneering connoisseur and collector of drawings who dabbled in etching as well as painting from at least as early as 1625, when he was sent to Italy to supervise the acquisition and transport to London of the Gonzaga collection. Rubens reported his presence in Antwerp in June 1628, which is probably where Van Dyck painted his magnificent portrait of Lanier. Lanier acquired this picture in the sale of the late King's goods for £10. The pose of his self-portrait reverses that in the Van Dyck, echoing it also in the vertical rock or ruined wall and drooping branches behind the sitter. According to Bellori, Van Dyck painted another portrait of Lanier (now untraceable) in the guise of David playing his harp before Saul. He is also thought to be depicted in Dobson's self-portrait with two others in the Northumberland Collection. He was also painted by Jan Lievens (engraved by Vorsterman), probably by Dobson and Isaac Oliver, and possibly by Guido Reni.

EC

10

William Dobson (1611–1646)

Portrait of a Musician, c.1644

Oil on canvas, 109.2 × 89.2 cm
Ferens Art Gallery, Hull

Malcolm Rogers, *William Dobson 1611–46* (NPG, London, 1983)

As with the Van Dyck portrait of Gage, here, too, Sir Oliver Millar was a pioneer in the field, organizing the first major exhibition devoted to Dobson at the Tate Gallery in 1951. When this portrait came up for auction a decade later, the Ferens Art Gallery obtained a grant to acquire it. It was then included in Malcolm Rogers's splendid exhibition at the National Portrait Gallery. There is, however, no evidence for the latter's supposition that this picture portrays either Nicholas Lanier or the composer Henry Lawes. (The name Nicholas Lanier is inscribed on a copy of the picture at Chillington but it resembles neither Van Dyck's magnificent portrait nor Jan Lievens's, nor indeed the self-portrait included in this exhibition [no. 9]). The outdoor setting features a relief depicting a lady perhaps singing from a book and another figure playing a lute in the background, and from this it has been deduced that the sitter is holding a scroll of music. The bust crowned with laurel on which the sitter quietly rests his hand is mysteriously familiar, most likely to be a poet, but is as yet unidentified.

John Aubrey was no doubt correct in defining Dobson as 'the most excellent painter that England hath yet bred'. At his best, as in both his portraits of the elderly Inigo Jones, Dobson rivals Van Dyck. Although he immediately succeeded and was clearly influenced by Van Dyck, who died on the eve of the Civil War, Dobson was a pupil of Francis Cleyn, and developed a more introspective style than Van Dyck. Like Van Dyck, he, too, died young at the peak of his powers, but his oeuvre was smaller (some 50–60 pictures with just a handful of full-lengths). His sitters were mainly Royalists, most of these residing at Oxford, which became the King's headquarters from 1643 until June 1646, when the city surrendered to Fairfax. EC

11

Robert Walker
(*c.* 1607– *c.*1658)
*Self-portrait, c.*1640–55

Oil on canvas, 73.7 × 70 cm
Ashmolean Museum, Oxford

Oliver Millar, *The Age of Charles I. Painting in England 1620–1649* (London, 1972), p. 102

John Sheeran, 'Robert Walker', in *The Dictionary of Art*, ed. Jane Turner, 33 vols. (London and New York, 1996), XXXII, p. 497

Although John Evelyn was pleased to be portrayed by 'Mr Walker that excellent Painter' (the picture is now in the National Portrait Gallery), modern art historians have not shared his enthusiasm, and research still needs to be done on Walker's work. During the Cromwellian era he performed the same function as Van Dyck had at the Caroline court, portraying the great and the good; but he was much less talented, and awkwardly drew attention to his deficiencies by recycling Van Dyck's portrait compositions. For example, his portrait of Richard Deane, General-at-Sea in the 1650s (National Maritime Museum), copies Van Dyck's design for a portrait of Charles I's Lord High Admiral, the Earl of Northumberland (Alnwick Castle); and many other instances could be detailed. The present picture may hint at the reasons for this campaign of seeming plagiarism. It is not a mere replica but an ironic reworking of Van Dyck's *Self-portrait with a Sunflower* [cf. no. 17]. In place of the sunflower Walker points at a statuette of Mercury, which has been read in different ways: one interpreter cites Mercury's role as god of thieves, another as divine patron of the arts. The allusion may be somewhat less particularized. As the gods' messenger Mercury was concerned with all sorts of mediation and transference (including commerce and theft); it is also the case that by the seventeenth century he had become associated with the art of painting (as in the allegorical picture by Goltzius, Frans Hals Museum, Haarlem). Walker may be pointing to Mercury in this plural guise, and, in a painting which inevitably recalls his own wholesale appropriation of Van Dyckian designs from a Caroline to a Cromwellian context, impudently invoking him as – let us say – the god of cultural transactions. Walker's plagiarisms may have had a conscious political purpose, as he boldly tried to remake the new élite in the image of the old. JP

12

Sir Peter Lely
(1618–1680)
*Henry Stone, c.*1648

Oil on canvas, 87.9 × 73 cm
National Portrait Gallery

'The Note-Book and Account Book of Nicholas Stone', ed. W.L, Spiers, (Walpole Society, VII, 1919)

Henry Stone (1616–1653) was the eldest son of England's most successful master mason and sculptor, Nicholas Stone, and his wife Maria, daughter of the Dutch architect Hendrik de Keyser. In 1635, Henry was sent to Holland to study painting with his uncle Thomas de Keyser. In the spring of 1638 he was joined in Paris by his younger brother Nicholas, and together they set off for a tour of France and Italy which the latter recorded in the most fascinating travel diary of the period. In Florence they copied pictures in the Uffizi, and chatted with Grand Duke Ferdinando II, who enquired after the collector Earl of Arundel and ordered his 'gallery keeper to deliver to my brother [Henry, to copy] any piece he should chuse'. In Rome they met Bernini, who enquired after the bust of Charles I he had made after Van Dyck's triple portrait. After a brief visit to Naples, the brothers returned to Rome, where they stayed for more than three years, sending their father casts, books and prints. On their return journey through Bologna they met Guido Reni, whose pictures the brothers would have seen in the royal collections. While Nicholas Stone Junior filled a sketchbook of architectural plans

and elevations, mainly of Florentine and Roman buildings, Henry filled an equivalently interesting one with landscape sketches and figure drawings. Both sketchbooks were acquired by John Talman and, via James Paine, ended up in Sir John Soane's Museum.

In 1643 the brothers returned to England, where Henry seems to have practised as a painter and copyist with some success, continuing to travel extensively. Vertue refers to this portrait, then in the collection of Mr Russell, as painted by Lely 'in his first manner'. It was engraved by Bannerman and published in Walpole's *Anecdotes of Painting* (1742), II, p. 31. It was sold as a Dobson in the 1960s but identified as a Lely by Sir Oliver Millar and acquired by the National Portrait Gallery as such in 1987. It had already been somewhat over-cleaned. Stone is depicted against a cliff-like background reminiscent of Van Dyck's *Nicholas Lanier* (and Lanier's *Self-portrait* [no. 9]). Like several Van Dyck portraits of artists, and Van der Borcht's of John Evelyn [no. 8], Stone holds a drawing in front of him, in this case pointing to it as if advertising his profession. A good, somewhat Dobsonesque, portrait of Thomas, Lord Leigh survives at Stoneleigh Abbey, Worcestershire, which is inscribed *H. Stone F. 1649*. Stone died in August 1653 and was buried in St Martin's-in-the-Fields, where a long inscription by his brother John described him as a 'painter and Statuary, who having passed the greatest part of 37 years in Holland France and Italy, acheaved a fair Renown for his Excellency in Artes and Languages ...'. EC

13

Mary Beale (1633–1699)
Charles Beale the Elder, c.1663

Oil on canvas, 24.1 × 21 cm
National Portrait Gallery

David Piper, *Catalogue of the Seventeenth-Century Portraits in the National Portrait Gallery* (London, 1963), p. 23

Richard Jeffree, Elizabeth Walsh, *The Excellent Mrs Mary Beale* (London, 1975)

Tabitha Barber, *Mary Beale: Portrait of a seventeenth-century painter, her family and her studio* (Geffrye Museum, London, 1999)

As well as being the earliest firmly attributed work by Mary Beale, this frank and intimate portrait is the earliest sketch in a long series of portraits of the artist's husband.

In what was an interesting role reversal for seventeenth-century gender relations, Beale's husband Charles (1632–1705) supported Beale in her career as a successful portrait painter. Acting as her assistant, he prepared materials, experimented with colour pigments and documented closely in his series of notebooks the progress of Mary's individual paintings and their business as a whole. Equality appears to have reigned in both the professional and domestic life of this couple, making it an extremely unusual marriage of the seventeenth century. This arrangement is undoubtedly revealed in the honest yet dignified manner in which Mary Beale has chosen to portray her husband in this portrait. Utilizing her close friendship with Sir Peter Lely, Mary Beale took informal tuition from this eminent artist. Unfortunately, this seems to have led to Beale compromising her own style and adopting elements of that of Lely, particularly in pose, in order to achieve the commercial success that enabled her to support her family financially. It is this particular criticism that has led, despite her having been well patronized within her own lifetime, to the subsequent decline of Beale's reputation. It is only, therefore, in portraits such as this, of family or friends, intended purely 'for study and improvement' and not profit, that we are able to see the true talent and capabilities of the most prolific female artist to have worked in England in the seventeenth century.

HONOR BEDDARD

14

John Michael Wright (1617–1694)

Sir William Bruce

Signed and dated 166[4]

Oil on canvas, 71.1 × 61 cm

Scottish National Portrait Gallery

J.G. Dunbar, *Sir William Bruce* (Scottish Arts Council, 1970)

Sara Stevenson and Duncan Thomson, *John Michael Wright: The King's Painter* (Scottish National Portrait Gallery, Edinburgh, 1982)

Albert J. Loomie, 'J.M. Wright's Visit to London in the Summer of 1655', *Burlington Magazine* (November 1987), p. 721

Sir William Bruce (1630–1710) of Kinross (where there is a later copy of this picture more clearly dated 1664), was the second son of Robert Bruce of Blairhall by his wife Catherine, daughter of Sir John Preston of Valleyfield. Bruce was Scotland's most distinguished gentleman-architect, being appointed Surveyor of the King's Buildings in Scotland in 1671, when he began rebuilding Holyrood House. He also designed his own impressively austere mansion at Kinross. According to the *Dictionary of National Biography*, '… no one in Scotland probably contributed more in a private capacity to bring about the restoration of the royal family, to whom he proved a firm and constant friend. He is said to have been the channel of communication between General Monk and the young king, and to have had the honour of first conveying to the latter the inclination of the former to serve him.' There indeed survives a passport signed by Monk permitting him to 'returne to Holland', where the King then was. Charles II rewarded Bruce soon after the Restoration with a knighthood and then in 1668 by creating him a baronet. In 1685–6 he was a member of the Privy Council of Scotland. Although the sitter is depicted with a realism more akin to Dobson than to Van Dyck's less close-up and more elongated figures, the feathery brushwork is closer to the Flemish master's and in this looks forward to Gainsborough's still greater affinity with Van Dyck's technique. Along the bottom of the canvas a strip of later canvas has been added and painted, probably with reference to the Kinross copy, to replace a strip that had been cut off. Bruce is wearing an Indian gown, a striped version of the type that Pepys acquired in order to sit to John Hayls in 1666.

EC

15

Sir Peter Lely (1618–1680) *Portrait of a Woman*, *c.*1670–5

Oil on canvas, 126.4 × 101.5 cm
Tate

C.H. Collins Baker, *Lely and the Stuart Portrait Painters*, 2 vols. (London, 1912), I, p. 173, repr. facing p. 176, and II, p. 128, no. 148, as 'Duchess of Portsmouth'

R.B. Beckett, *Lely* (London, 1951), p. 58, no. 421, as 'Duchess of Portsmouth'

Lely's debt to Van Dyck is seen in the seated three-quarter-length composition, with a richly patterned curtain billowing down to the right, and a stone window opening at the left with an empty vase on its ledge. The sitter rests her left hand on a golden object, perhaps echoing the jar that symbolized the reformed sinner Mary Magdalene. Through the window is a landscape, with buildings on a wooded hill and a stretch of water below.

The sitter cannot be identified with certainty. While a deep decolletage is seen in many female portraits by Lely, it is unusual for him to depict a woman with a breast fully exposed, as here. His best-known portrait of this type is the so-called *Diana Kirke* (British Art Center, New Haven). Another example is known only from the surviving engraving, identified as 'The Lady Williams' (Beckett, p.66, no. 567). This manner of portrayal probably denotes a mistress, rather than a lady of impeccable chastity.

Recent conservation has revealed a later inscription, *Dutchess of Cleveland*, on the ledge centre left, enabling the work to be identified in a 1769 inventory of the contents of Combe Abbey, Warwickshire. It hung in the Green Damask Bedchamber and was paired with a portrait of the 'Duke of Ormond', also by Lely (Craven Papers, Bodleian Library, transcribed in Willem-Jan Hoogsteder, *De schilderijen van Frederik en Elizabeth, Konig en Konigin van Bohemen*, PhD thesis, Utrecht, 1986). Similar inscriptions, some incorrect, appear on other portraits from Combe Abbey and were probably added for the 5th Baron Craven (1705–1769).

Barbara Villiers, Countess of Castlemaine (1640–1709; created Duchess of Cleveland in August 1670) was Charles II's mistress from about 1660. Although Lely painted her many times, the present subject seems too youthful to be her. Collins Baker re-identified the sitter as the mistress who supplanted Cleveland in Charles's affections, the French-born Louise de Kerouaille (1649–1734). The resemblance to authentic portraits of Louise is not, however, strong.

When acquired by the Tate Gallery in 1965, the sitter was once again re-identified, this time as Margaret Hughes (died 1719), one of the first female stage-actors and the mistress of Charles II's cousin Prince Rupert. Rupert bequeathed his chattels to William, 1st Baron and Earl of Craven (1608–1697) in trust jointly for Margaret and his daughter by her, Ruperta, and paintings from Rupert's collection are subsequently recorded at Combe Abbey. The sitter stretches out her hand to quieten an adoring spaniel, and spaniels were closely identified with the Stuart royal family. However, comparison with a documented portrait of 'Madam Hewse' (private collection; Beckett 1951, pl. 109) is not conclusive.

Although most of the painting is in excellent condition, the lady's blue mantle may in the past have lost a thin top glaze of more intense blue, perhaps made of the costly pigment ultramarine, so that what is now seen is probably the under-layer. KAREN HEARN

16

Sir Peter Lely

Self-portrait, c.1675

Inscribed in a later hand:
Sir Peter Lely painted by himself
Oil on canvas, 76.2 × 63.5 cm
Private collection, London

David Piper, *Catalogue of the Seventeenth-Century Portraits in the National Portrait Gallery* (London, 1963), p. 201: mentioned in the collection of the Osborne family, who had been friends of Lely

Dryden remarked of Lely that he 'drew many graceful pictures, but few of them were like … because he always studied himself more than those who sat to him' (*Sylvae*, 1685), recalling the famous criticism of Pepys – a friend of the painter – that 'Mr Lilly' was 'a mighty proud man and full of state'.

A great interest in oneself, however, is a virtue in self-portraits, and Lely's rank amongst his most penetrating works. They chart the painter from youth and his first arrival in England – as in *Self-portrait playing the Lute* (private collection) – through prosperous maturity in the National Portrait Gallery *Self-portrait* to old age in this example. Though his aspect is no less magnificent than in the works of the 1660s, bravado has been superseded by introspection. There is a tradition that by the late 1670s Lely was disturbed by the encroachment on his dignity and practice of the young Kneller, and certainly there is little sense of ease in this image. Lely, who was also a great collector, clearly felt that there could be no rest from his work, and was to die in 1680 of a stroke whilst at his easel.

Stylistically, this painting, which has descended in the Osborne family – friends and patrons of Lely – bears all the hallmarks of Lely's late manner. By comparison with the *Self-portrait with Hugh May* (Audley End) it can be dated to the later 1670s, when the painter's style became looser. Brown tonality and free, dry brushwork predominate, and compositionally he makes a more frequent use of the elaborate *faux*-architectural cartouche. JAMES MULRAINE

17

After Van Dyck
Self-portrait with a Sunflower

Oil on canvas, 63.5 × 63.5 cm
Private collection, London

Christopher Brown and Hans Vlieghe, *Van Dyck 1599–1641* (Antwerp and London, 1999), pp. 244–5

This copy of a famous and enigmatic self-portrait by Van Dyck seems to date from the eighteenth, or possibly the late seventeenth, century. The original composition has an oblong format; this square format resembles a print made after it by Wenceslaus Hollar, and an eighteenth-century painted copy at Ham House.

The original possibly dates from 1633; in April of that year the Lord Chamberlain issued a warrant 'for a Chain and a Medal of One Hundred and Ten Pounds value to be presented unto Sir Anthony Vandyck'. The medal would have borne the King's head, and the chain was no doubt a reward for the first year of Van Dyck's service; gold chains had become customary gifts from rulers to court artists. The portrait therefore alludes to Van Dyck's success as 'Principal Painter to their Majesties', and the sunflower, which follows the sun's course through the sky as if with a continual gaze, would appropriately symbolize his special relationship with the sovereign, to whose features he had to devote a sustained professional scrutiny. At the same time the symbolism has a wider import. Van Dyck does not display the medal with the King's head, but holds up the gold chain as if it had more general associations; and the motif had been a significant one in the repertoire of European symbolism since antiquity. The sunflower, by contrast, was new to Europe, having arrived from South America only about seventy years before, but it had already taken on a symbolic identity. Because it matched the human scale, and seemed (from its reaction to the sun) to share some of the sensitivities of human nature, it was a ready object of symbolic fantasy. Even the botanists who first recorded it were prone to view it anthropomorphically, and emblem writers loaded it with meaning: it figured the lover yearning for the light of love, either human or divine, the soul seeking illumination, and so on. As the sunflower's double in this portrait, Van Dyck places himself beyond the confines of the court, out in the world at large (the chain evokes the concatenated organization of the universe), and suggests the painter's work is to exercise the faculty of vision as best he may, to be a seer of the natural order and what lies beyond it. JP

18

Style of Van Dyck

Oliver Cromwell

Oil on canvas, 127 × 101.5 cm
National Maritime Museum, Greenwich

Concise Catalogue of the Oil Paintings in the National Maritime Museum, (Woodbridge, 1988), p. 411

Laura Lunger Knoppers, *Constructing Cromwell. Ceremony, Portrait and Print 1645–1661* (Cambridge, 2000)

This portrait has been implausibly attributed to Robert Walker. It is a visual confection dating from the late seventeenth or the eighteenth century. The head is ultimately derived from a well-known image of Cromwell by the miniaturist Samuel Cooper (D. Foskett, *Samuel Cooper and His Contemporaries* [London, 1974], p. 19). The armoured body comes from Van Dyck's portrait of *James, Marquess of Hamilton* (E. Larsen, *The Paintings of Anthony van Dyck*, 2 vols. (Freren, 1988), II, p. 336). The background vista, which shows a cavalry skirmish, a fortified town and ships possibly exchanging hostile fire, may be paraphrased from the Walker portrait of Cromwell in the National Portrait Gallery, which in the background has ships and troops embarking. It might also be a composite invention, like the portrait figure, summing up the dangers which faced the Commonwealth and Protectorate: the arms painted on the right are those of the Protectorate, with the motto '*Pax quaeritur bello*' (Through war is sought peace). The conflation of Van Dyck with Cooper, who portrayed many Cromwellian notables, may suggest an evolving portrait tradition not too fussed about political allegiances; but we need to know the provenance and purpose of a picture like this before coming to such a conclusion. JP

19

Enoch Seeman (c.1690–1745)

Self-portrait, c.1709

Oil on canvas, 63.5 × 45.7 cm
Private collection, London

Seeman's reputation among contemporary painters is of one more competent than outstanding, a judgment based upon his later portraits when, comfortable with royal patronage, he adopted a generalized version of the prevailing London manner.

His earlier works, however, display greater animation and virtuosity, as this *Self-portrait* demonstrates. It recalls Walpole's reference (*Anecdotes*, II, p. 294) to 'his own portrait in the finical manner of [Balthasar] Denner', whose work was then in vogue on the Continent. The strong chiaroscuro casts our attention on to the sitter's bright, engaging eyes, smooth skin and elegantly lit hair, startling characteristics which become standardized and abstracted in the later portraits.

Seeman was brought to England by his father, the Flemish painter Enoch Seeman the Elder, in 1704, and by 1708 was already executing the ambitious *Colonel Andrew Bisset and his family.* This painting is Seeman's earliest known work in this country, but also contains his earliest known self-portrait, for a shadowy figure in the background, long believed to be a posthumous representation of the Colonel's son, bears features clearly comparable with the present *Self-portrait.* In confirmation of this, the figure gestures towards a pedestal on which is inscribed *Enoch Seeman. Pinx. AE. 18. 1708.* JM

20

Sir Godfrey Kneller Bt. (1646–1723)

Self-portrait, 1719

Signed and dated 171(?9)
Oil on canvas, 76 × 63.5 cm
Private collection, London

Dalya Alberge, 'Art Market', *The Independent*, 21 May 1991

Private correspondence with J. Douglas Stewart

Re-examination of the inscription on this newly discovered portrait now suggests that it dates 1719 rather than to 1710 as previously believed. It becomes, therefore, a fascinating private glimpse of Kneller in his final years and stands among his last and strongest self-portraits.

Unlike many earlier examples it is relatively informal. Works such as the Kit-Cat *Self-portrait* of about 1706–11 (National Portrait Gallery) or the *Self-portrait with Lady Kneller* of around 1715–20 (private collection) show Kneller not so much an artist but rather a gentleman, distinguishable from many of his clients only by the gold chain and medal that he received from King William III. Here, however, he is not reinforced by the symbols of status, and appears informally. The only trace of his position is the portrait's air of stern dignity and the suggestion of a paint-brush under his right arm. The absence of his gold chain may be explained both by the intimacy of the image and by the fact, perhaps, that the wearing of such objects may have begun to seem excessive in the incipient Age of Taste.

Given these circumstances it is excusable that the sitter was long believed to be William Hogarth, since the painting displays the vigorous brushwork, directness and lack of pretension that is associated with his style. For the student of Kneller, however, the correct identification is an excellent opportunity to refute any suggestion that Kneller's later years showed a dwindling of his powers. As a piece of painting it is as assured as any that Kneller produced, and it has –as Malcolm Rogers has observed (private correspondence) – greater psychological acuity than other self-portraits. As a composition it is, in the sitter's dominance of the picture plane, as good a resolution of the half-length as exists. JM

21

Jonathan Richardson (1665–1745)

Self-portrait as a writer, c.1735

Oil on canvas, 91.4 × 66 cm
Private collection, London

Carol Gibson-Wood, *Jonathan Richardson, Art Theorist of the English Enlightenment* (New Haven and London, 2000), pp. 41 (ill.), 42

Even if Jonathan Richardson did not enjoy a fuller intellectual life than other painters of his time, he has, however, left the greatest trace of his literary and philosophical interests. Indeed, by the late eighteenth century his painting was seen as a sideshow; his legacy was the fostering of connoisseurship, both through his unequalled collection of Old Master drawings and through his 1715 *Theory of Painting*, in which he advanced an intellectual method for the appreciation of pictures.

The evident quality of this present portrait, with its vigorous and luminous draperies and boldly modelled face, proves that Richardson's talents as a painter were of a higher order than posterity remembered. It is significant, though, that he depicts himself not as an artist but as a writer. By the 1730s Richardson had retired from practice. Encouraged by Alexander Pope, he was undertaking a number of projects associated with Milton, such as *Explanatory Notes and Remarks on Milton's 'Paradise Lost'*, which Richardson and his son published in 1734.

Richardson saw his task as that of emphasizing the righteousness and high moral reputation of the poet with whom he identified and to whom he attributed his own virtues. In this context *Self-portrait as a writer* is a manifesto, an impression heightened by the textual pointers to the writer's – and, as he thought, the poet's – philosophy. The stone on which he leans is labelled *solidity* whilst the ray of light appearing from the left contains the words *What shall be, Must.* JM

22

Thomas Gainsborough RA (1727–1788)

Self-portrait as a boy, c.1739

Oil on paper laid on to canvas, 22.9 × 20.3 cm
Private collection, London

Adrienne Corri, 'Gainsborough's Early Career', *Burlington Magazine* (April 1983), frontispiece

Rica Jones, *Notes on the Technical Examination*, 1990 (unpublished)

John Gage, *Colour and Culture* (London, 1993), p. 180, note 33

Michael Rosenthal, *The Art of Thomas Gainsborough* (New Haven and London, 1999), p. 5 (illus.)

William Vaughan, *Gainsborough* (forthcoming London, 2002)

This painting of the thirteen-year-old Gainsborough descends from the Butcher family, stewards to the Duke of Bedford and agents between the artist and the Duke. Self-portraits by any painter of this age are a considerable rarity; such an early glimpse of one of British painting's most prolific and accomplished artists is of exceptional interest.

It is recognised that Gainsborough was practising painting at an impressively young age. The painter himself refers to this in a letter to Henry Bate concerning *Cornards Wood* (National Gallery), in which he explains that the landscape – 'a little in the schoolboy stile' – was 'begun before I left school'. It has recently been established that Gainsborough was receiving payments – made via his father – from the Fonnereau family of Suffolk as early as 1736. Although the precise commission to which these payments relate is not established, the Fonnereaus were also patrons of the painter Francis Hayman, with whom Gainsborough was associated when he moved to London in 1739.

In style and likeness the *Self-portrait* conforms entirely to Gainsborough. There is a strong facial resemblance to the artist as shown in the *Self-portrait with Wife and Daughter* of about 1748, which is the second earliest recorded self-portrait. In execution it foreshadows the later self-portraits by the concentration of light that distinguishes the head and by the sitter's directness and intensity of gaze. The doll-like anatomy is parallelled in many of Gainsborough's earliest portraits. It also displays a precocious use of Gainsborough's hallmark glazing in the modelling of the coat – a distinction which sets him apart from most contemporary portraitists. JM

23
William Hogarth after Van Dyck
Inigo Jones, 1757

Oil on canvas, 91.5 × 71 cm
National Maritime Museum, Greenwich

Concise Catalogue of the Oil Paintings in the National Maritime Museum (Woodbridge, 1988), p. 209

Ronald Paulson, *Hogarth*, 3 vols. (Cambridge, 1993), III, p. 270

This was painted in 1757 for Sir Edward Littleton, whose country house, Teddesley Hall in Staffordshire, was being remodelled in a neo-classical style. Inigo Jones (1573–1652) was regarded as the founding father of English neo-classicism because of his promotion of the architecture of Palladio, a cause taken up again in the eighteenth century by Lord Burlington.

The portrait is ultimately based on an original drawing by Van Dyck, owned by Burlington and now at Chatsworth, which Hogarth knew through an engraving by Robert van Voerst. He seems to have studied Van Dyck's image carefully: certain minor but subtle alterations show him developing the design in his own way. He diminishes the number of buttons on the jacket, and slightly loosens the collar just where it joins at the top, marking this with a crumpled meandering line of white paint. He indents the profile of the curtain, which Van Dyck had made straight, and introduces deep extra diagonal folds into the curtain and Jones's cloak below it. He also makes the paper fold across the middle. These added indentations register with an increased physicality the jut of Jones's elbow and the tilt of his head. At the same time the tension of his gaze slightly relaxes. The rhythms of the design become broader, more Baroque – very Hogarthian, but perhaps not in accord with the patron's neo-classical taste. JP

24 (overleaf)
Thomas Gainsborough after Anthony van Dyck
Lord Bernard Stuart, 1760s

Oil on canvas, 73.7 × 59.7 cm
Trustees of Gainsborough's House, Sudbury, Suffolk

Exhibition of Paintings and Drawings by Thomas Gainsborough, RA (Cincinnati Art Museum, May 1931), no. 45, plate 16

E. K. Waterhouse, *Gainsborough* (London, 1958), no. 1018

Gainsborough's work frequently reveals his debt to Van Dyck, a fact he acknowledged in his last words: 'We are all going to Heaven, and Van Dyck is of the party'. He copied a number of Van Dyck's paintings and often used prints after the seventeenth-century artist's work to inform his compositions. The portrait of the Stuart brothers [fig. 1] particularly fascinated him and he must have enjoyed access to the original, as no print of the painting is known. It seems unlikely that he travelled to Cobham in Kent to see the portrait and he probably copied it in Lord Darnley's London house in the mid 1760s.

Gainsborough painted a full-size copy of the whole double portrait, a picture which Lord Darnley bought at the artist's posthumous sale in 1789 (St Louis Art Museum). He sought further instruction from it and made smaller copies of each head. In the copy exhibited Gainsborough simplifies the colours and shapes by heightening the contrasts in

the silk cloak and hair and using the ground to provide the mid tones. The comparison between the two paintings is instructive; it provides an insight into the lessons learned by Gainsborough from his seventeenth-century hero. HUGH BELSEY

25

Thomas Gainsborough RA

Self-portrait, c.1787

Oil on canvas, 74.9 × 61 cm
Royal Academy of Arts (presented by Margaret Gainsborough, the painter's daughter, in 1808)

E.K. Waterhouse, *Gainsborough* (London, 1958), p. 69, no.292

This portrait may be seen as the fulfilment of the potential displayed in Gainsborough's early *Self-portrait* [no. 22]. Sternness and humour are combined in the raised brow and the ironic twist of the mouth, but the elements common to his earlier self-portraits, the lighting around the head and the level, direct gaze are also apparent.

This painting, which is probably unfinished, shows Gainsborough's late London manner at its most assured: apparently careless strokes construct the image with great force and acuity, whilst a masterful suggestion of light powerfully evokes the sitter's presence.

This portrait was intended by Gainsborough for his friend the musician Carl Friedrich Abel, which establishes the self-portrait in the context of an intimate, almost 'speaking', gift from one artist to another. Abel sadly did not live to receive the painting, as he died in 1787, but Gainsborough regarded it as the truest image of himself. In the following year – the year of his death – he stated that he wished no posthumous representation to be made of him in any medium save, if desired, an engraving from the present portrait. JM

PHOTOGRAPHIC CREDITS

Fig. 1, cat. nos. 4, 7 :
© National Gallery, London;
Fig. 4, cat. nos. 1, 5, 8, 12, 13:
by courtesy of the National Portrait Gallery, London;
Cat. no. 10: by courtesy of the Ferens Art Gallery, Hull;
Cat. no. 11 :
Ashmolean Museum, Oxford;
Cat. no. 14:
Scottish National Portrait Gallery;
Cat. no. 15: © Tate, London;
Cat. nos. 18, 23: © National Maritime Museum, London;
Cat. no. 24: by courtesy of Trustees of Gainsborough's House, Sudbury, Suffolk;
Cat. no. 25: by courtesy of Royal Academy of Arts, London.

This catalogue is published to accompany the exhibition *The Stuart Portrait: Status and Legacy,* curated by Professor Edward Chaney and Godfrey Worsdale.

Generous financial assistance has been received from Southampton Institute.

The catalogue has been prepared by Paul Holberton and is published by Southampton City Art Gallery in association with Southampton Institute.

Southampton City Art Gallery staff:
Tim Craven
Mary Kilpatrick
John Lawrence
Lauren McCrisken
Esta Mion-Jones
Rebecca Moisan
Godfrey Worsdale

Southampton City Art Gallery
Civic Centre
Southampton SO14 7LP
Tel +44 (0)23 8083 2277
Fax +44 (0)23 8083 2153
Email art.gallery@southampton.gov.uk

Published by order of Southampton City Art Gallery, 2001

ISBN 0 901723 27 4

Edited by Edward Chaney and Godfrey Worsdale

Designed by Roger Davies
daviesdesign@onetel.net.uk
www.rogerdaviesdesign.co.uk

Printed in Italy

Paul Holberton publishing

SOUTHAMPTON CITY COUNCIL

SOUTHAMPTON INSTITUTE